# Praise for *Trailing the Azimuth*

"Whether you are an explorer, spiritual contemplative, or poetry lover craving a glimpse into the mystical beauty of life, you owe it to yourself to take this enchanting journey. . . . Threads of light and hope skillfully weave the natural with the supernatural, and I felt refreshed and uplifted."

—D. K. REED, AUTHOR OF *THE STONES OF BOTHYNUS* TRILOGY

"Trailing the Azimuth plumbs the deep complexities of being Appalachian, both inside and outside of Appalachia—a passionate exploration of beauty that ultimately transcends any region. Dodson's is a fresh yet familiar voice. She has delivered here an extraordinary first collection of poems that will resonate long after the last one has been read."

—AMY GREENE, AUTHOR OF *BLOODROOT*

"Part travelogue, part book of psalms, part meditation on a world-shaking pandemic, this collection reminds us of 'the responsibility to remember,' to '[bring] to light / the gold of buried knowledge.' Dodson does so with keen observation and musicality, spiritual centeredness and mindfulness, and a deep love of place and culture. . . . After so much pandemic darkness and despair, this book offers its readers love and light."

—GARY J. WHITEHEAD, AUTHOR OF *STRANGE WHAT RISES*

"Written in the spirit of a travel journal, these poems capture what it might be like to walk alongside Dodson on the trail. The reader is immediately struck with the union of the 'here and now,' the 'what once was,' and the 'what lies beyond.' . . . Dodson possesses a keen eye and perceptive lyrics, both of which are on full display here."

—PAUL E. REED, University of Alabama

"The wisdom of Dodson's words resonates in her soft attention to the nature, people, and wildlife of southern Appalachia and elsewhere. Familiar, song-like rhythms mix with clear images to compose poems that both dazzle and inspire awe. This collection embodies learning, looking, and each love that surrounds the speaker, and by extension, us."

—CHRISTINA SEYMOUR, author of When Is a Burning Tree

# Trailing the Azimuth

# Trailing the Azimuth

DANITA DODSON

RESOURCE *Publications* · Eugene, Oregon

TRAILING THE AZIMUTH

Resource Publications
An Imprint of Wipf and Stock Publishers
199 W. 8th Ave., Suite 3
Eugene, OR 97401

www.wipfandstock.com

PAPERBACK ISBN: 978-1-6667-3176-7
HARDCOVER ISBN: 978-1-6667-2464-6
EBOOK ISBN: 978-1-6667-2465-3

11/03/21

*For Alfred Clarence Dodson,*
*my father and my friend,*
*who introduced me to literature,*
*who blazed a forest trail so I could walk,*
*and who always imagined that one day*
*I would sing my life in lines*

# Contents

Contents

## Wayfarer's Psalms

## Pandemic Pathways

# Thanksgivings

My experiences have been richly diverse, and for that I am immensely blessed and grateful. My mother used to say that I have "many irons in the fire," using an old Appalachian expression. My Latinx friends tell me that I wear "muchos sombreros." While both maxims are apt, I prefer the metaphor of "trails" to describe my multifaceted walks through life. Perhaps this cherished symbol has, in part, to do with my passion for recognizing footpaths as I hike. However, neither literally nor figuratively do I consider myself a trailblazer. I simply have been lured to roads already existing, though ones not frequently travelled, and I have taken them—which, as poet Robert Frost reminds us, most often makes "all the difference."[1] Since the poems in *Trailing the Azimuth* could not have been possible without the remarkable opportunities and insights that others have given me, I wish to acknowledge some of the inspiring guides of the journey.

I give special thanks to my nephew, Caleb Seals, who inspired the title of this book in one of our coffee conversations, during which he described how he had navigated the wilderness in military field exercises, using a compass and a map to chart the *azimuth*—in other words, to find bearings in the puzzling wild and to seek the direction toward which to walk. The symbol of the azimuth is woven into the fabric of the book, representing the trajectories for both physical journeys and those allegorical ones that we all must make through the wildernesses of life.

My deep gratitude goes to the Ahimsa Center at California State Polytechnic University, Pomona—especially Drs. Tara Sethia and Christian Bracho—for the inspiration in nonviolence.

I am indebted to the National Endowment for the Humanities, the New Mexico History Museum, the Crow Canyon Archaeological

---

1. "The Road Not Taken," public domain

Center, and the Mesa Verde National Park for the opportunities to serve as a humanities fellow in the Southwest. Thanks also for the hospitality of the Taos Pueblo, the Santo Domingo Pueblo, and the Navajo Nation.

My appreciation goes to the University of Arizona's Center for Middle Eastern Studies *Teach Turkey* program and the U.S. Department of Education, which allowed me to serve as a Fulbright-Hays fellow in Turkey. Thanks also to my program colleagues and the people of Turkey.

I am beholden to the University of Mobile, and especially Dr. Hazel Petersen, who gave me the chance to teach at its Latin American Campus in San Marcos, Carazo, Nicaragua, during the last two years of Violeta Chamorro's peaceful leadership. I am thankful for the people of Nicaragua, with whom I am still linked closely in friendship and communication, even amid their present adversities under a violent dictatorship.

My gratitude is extended to the Tennessee Education Association, the Children's Defense Fund-Alex Haley Farm, and the Green McAdoo Cultural Center for the opportunity to speak and to learn at the *Keep Walking* workshop, which is honored in "Walking in Clinton."

I give thanks to the Highlander Research and Education Center in New Market, Tennessee, for continuing the work and the conversations of Myles Horton and Paulo Freire, whose book *We Make the Road by Walking* is mentioned in "Mecca to Monteagle." Thanks also to the kind gentleman who let me inside the old Highlander Folk School but whose name I never learned.

Special thanksgiving is uplifted for my close-knit family, my friends near and far, and my church. I also give tribute to my homeplace of Sneedville, Tennessee, with its natural beauty, kind people, and diverse culture—which includes Cherokee, Melungeon, and Scotch-Irish heritage.

I am grateful for the wisdom and memory of the departed: my mother, Joyce Dodson; my best friend, Pam Brewer; my grandparents and their ancestors; and the literary trailblazers mentioned in my poems—Whitman, Thoreau, Yeats, Hafiz, Tolstoy, Hughes, and Darío.

I give a special thanks to several author-friends—Amy Greene, D.K. Reed, Gary J. Whitehead, Paul E. Reed, and Christina Seymour—for their inspiration, encouragement, and endorsement of this book.

My heartfelt gratitude flows to Matthew Wimer, George Callihan, Savanah N. Landerholm, and all the nice folks at Wipf and Stock for bringing this book to life.

I utter a profound prayer of thanksgiving to the good Lord, especially for granting me the grace to witness and to communicate the beauty of all Creation.

Finally, I give thanks to all of you, my readers. May you find threads of kinship in these poems, and may you be inspired to speak the wonder that you behold as you traverse your own paths.

# Tennessee Trails

# These Tennessee Woods

In these Tennessee woods
filled with dampness and birdsong,
teeming space of ephemeral growth
and eternal evanescence,
conscious of cyclical wheels
turning to begin and to end again,
I commune with Being,
with trillium in an emergent forest,
with dogwood crosses
murmuring the truth of rebirth.

As the spring breath blows softly
upon the woodland labyrinth
like a remembered promise,
quickening the slumbering soil,
returning verdant kindness
to the waiting branches,
        in surprise
the unexpected orchids arrive—
common once in an older day
but now forgotten, endangered—
pink blessings in hundreds
of pairs of a lady's slippers,
poised ready to amble, to ramble,
rare beauty in this protected space
cultivated simply by walking.

To these Tennessee woods,
I take you too, even in your absence.
To the trillium and to the orchids,
I carry you in my core, in my breath,
bringing you as to a sanctuary.

# Clinch Mountain Overlook

The blue crests of Clinch Mountain stand
like towers above the perfumed valley,
eddying the redbud's newborn breath
over the vanished site of old Bean Station,
once a bustling frontier outpost
that spread its friendly arms to greet
feisty long hunters, hopeful immigrants,
and pilgrims on a path.

From this crest rose Daniel Boone's shouts
as he moved blithely with the wind,
notching trees to trace the cleft
in the green knolls, a Cumberland Gap
on the Wilderness Road, the trail west,
stopping with fellow travelers to drink
at silver streams, to gaze at rhododendron,
to embrace apertures.

And the old paths of the azure ridges hold
the folksy hoofmarks of Davy Crockett,
volunteer son of these mountains,
whose name and memory blaze
boulevards and stadiums,
whose family tavern still sits
beyond the lough, its logs engraved
with trekkers' tales.

Perhaps only the hemlocks remember
an earlier trace, the Warrior's Path,
where native feet followed buffalo steps,
learned where springs and salt licks lay,
and trailed the sunlit natural passes
through colossal rocks,
fearless in spite of wildcats
howling in the darkness.

The earth surely recalls these sundry tracks,
the deep furrows and the green angles
holding place and remembrance.
The wind surely whispers the distant time
before TVA flooded the ancestral farms
in the lush valley to carve an epic lake
that was christened the *Cherokee*,
at once remembering and erasing old trails.

As I sit on the summit alone, I almost think
I can hear footsteps and wagons, weaving
a resolute cadence as they seek bearings,
following the earth's quilt and their dreams,
embracing refuge or retreat,
and only the hums of Highway 25E,
as it curls in route behind me,
remind me of my distance.

# Message in the Soil

Tilling the earth
one spring day, upturning
stones and daisies
and silty lumps of clay,
I chanced upon my old
Cherokee Spirit,
now only a broken
and battered shard buried
too long under centuries
of forgetfulness.

As I removed the dust
and perhaps the blood
from this blunt fragment
of time and heritage,
caressing the crevices
long gone untouched,
I discovered a simple
flint piece, once shaped
and focused and spent.

This message in the soil
speaks to me, laying bare
the path of an ancestor,
a Tsalagi wayfarer
who traipsed this land,

making heavier treads
with moccasin feet
than I can possibly make
with new lugged boots
on a Clingman's Dome.

Still, the missive confirms,
inviting me to the journey.
*Eladi edasdi.* Walk.

# Clinch River Song

Roving in the viridescence,
      coursing leisurely
on this errant kayak,
I float like an eternal plan
      upon the old river
in the depths of my forest world,
      my ancient wilderness,
        my heart.

Drifting along where
      even the diverse species
      of mussels
have a home,
      endangered elsewhere
        but safe here,
vagabonds gather strength,
      and losing the way
        means finding it.

This ambling liquid highway
      was dubbed the *Clinch*
when an Irishman—drowning—
begged his kindred explorers,
      "Clinch me!"
And we did, body and name.

To the river that remembers
salvation,
  I invite all souls
who wander
  who thirst
    who dare
to come and clinch peace.

# People of the Legend

People of the Legend, Nomads of the Myth,
we remember our Melungeon ancestors
who birthed the frontier in this place
where mystery still is as dense as the fog
upon the purple peaks of Powell Mountain,
which we see rising parallel to our Ridge.

Already the day of our elders is fading,
their voices melting into the gloaming,
floating down winding mountain paths,
dissolving before they reach the earth,
raveled like the seams of homespun quilts
worn and battered by time and moths.
Just as the jade glow of summer falls feyly
to October frost, crushed by the tramping
of boots on the route that brought them
to these hills, our ancestors' stories
and their steps will die with *us*, we fear,
so we must speak *them*.

They once burrowed through the wilderness,
settling Newman's Ridge before Tennessee
was a name on a map, trusting the healing
source of woodland herbs and cool streams.
They were called to a remote landscape
that would be their Eden, a hilltop sanctuary.

They found it with many inborn compasses,
listening closely to the Portuguese mariners
in their souls that embraced languid waters,
heeding the Moorish poets in their hearts
that named them singers of garden ghazals.

Sephardic? African? Turkish? Powhatan?
Maybe we are all, or perhaps none, of these.
Though our ancestral blood can be traced,
reflecting DNA paths of homelands far,
the truth of our lore is nestled in the graves
shrouded by the vines of rambling plants.
Scholars have flocked to our hills, blazing
their own routes, writing our blood in books,
seeking the history rewritten in our veins.
Still, our origins are supposed—invented.

Yet we walk forward, seeking the sunrise,
not willing to be marginalized by mystery,
embracing anew our multiracial heritage
as the descendant People of the Legend,
suffused in long winding trails.

# Language of the Hill Folk

The crinkle-crunch of fall's foliage
shatters summer's slumber.
The silence of sultry sky is awakened
by the brisk snap of crushed maple,
the languid leaves underfoot.

The wordless carpet of velvet moss
is quickened by the dripping sap
of yellowed pine in autumnal equinox.

The tractor purrs in the faded field,
humming a harvest valediction,
mowing down the last corn stalks
for fodder shocks to feed the cattle
lowing lyrically in the waning sun.

As tobacco cures on groaning planks
in the rickety, old, gray barn,
we gather in community at a stir-off,
absorbing the aromas and the sounds
of molasses boiling in a metal vat
while upon the wind we overhear
the cacophonous caws of crows.

Then we listen mutely in calm wonder,
pausing at this blessed ingathering,

felled by fall, stilled by gratitude.

Though our words abound at times,
and we speak aplenty amid our labors,
expressing life in our archaic words,
plangent parlance, and bluegrass rifts,
looking lovingly to the quilted hills
that are both *yourn* and mine,

sometimes we are simply silent
and let the earth do the talking for us.

# Patchwork of Remembrance

Memories, like homemade quilts made
for everyday use from necessity and love,
spread benevolently over my being,
each stitch a trail to who I am, a vein
of life offering warmth on wintry nights,
pulsing calico sunniness to my awakening.

The entwined laughter and tears of the years
smell pervasively of the cedar-box love
that protects the embroidery of smiles,
that preserves the basting of heartaches—
a patchwork of knowing, of acceptance.

Familial ties, thick and thin, topsy turvy,
blood and water, flannel and silk, all
are sewn into the fabric of ordinary days,
gathered both by accident and by fate,
shaped by the needle that sometimes jabs,
tugged by the thread that always ties.

# The Trails of Thomas

Thomas travelled many trails—but, at first,
he never trekked far from Bull Mountain,
land laced with staurolite fairy stones,
shaped like crosses, natural like his faith
in Jesus, the green earth, and his wife Mary.
He'd never left the Blue Ridge shadows
of that weathered old mountain range,
standing like a promise softened by time,
so he stayed and he prayed among
the rhododendrons of Goblintown Creek,
a silver branch like a healing web of tears
upon the broken-rock face of Virginia soil.
In peace he and *hisn* were sung to sleep
by nuthatches and yellow-throated warblers.
Like the father who tilled the nearby farm,
he was cut from the Blue Ridge earth,
planting and living and singing by the signs.
But sorrow came to his family, and Thomas
buried that father high on Bull Mountain,
then soon after laid to rest the little Frances,
who died of dysentery, redheaded daughter
still asleep today in the staurolite land—
her tiny bones interwoven with fairy stones.
His heart was heavy, and Mary
mirrored his soul and said, *Let's start anew.*

On the Great Wagon Road near the Mayo,
Thomas began the long oxcart journey
with Mary, their kids, a mother, and siblings
to a blue-green place in a Tennessee *holler*,
where he built a log cabin, hewing by hand
a ceiling joist from one tree, creating a kind
abode along Big Creek of the Clinch River.
But in a decade, deep grief came again,
peace toppled by violence and loss
when the Civil War cruelty came to the hills.
Veiled guerrillas charged into his home,
sought to coerce Thomas into the fight,
Confederates draped head to toe in sheets,
eye-holes cut out, so alien their form
until he glimpsed a neighbor's muddy boots.
His heart was heavy, and Mary
mirrored his soul and said, *Let's start anew.*

So Thomas, the pacifist preacher, parceled
a horse in the cover of night, fleeing the gray
peril, daring another exodus toward a place
he'd heard they'd be safe, navigating
his wife and children on the long, perilous
Wilderness Road toward Kentucky,
risking raiders who robbed them outright.
Hungry, weary, and poor—they didn't stop
until they reached the town of Manchester,
near the Goose Creek River and the salt lick,
aided by strangers who didn't coerce,
who let them earn their keep 'til they found
the means to farm a piece of Kentucky land.
They stayed there ten years, but Tennessee

loomed like a full moon inside Thomas.
His heart was heavy, and Mary
mirrored his soul and said, *Let's start anew.*

Like an exiled Odysseus ten years at sea,
Thomas uttered prayers for restoration,
returning with his family to that log cabin
in a remote Tennessee holler, embracing
a landscape no longer at war, finding
again the stalwart space that had stood
in love and sorrow, in sun and snow,
still holding the echoes of cries and songs,
a home waiting vacant like a hopeful mother
expecting the arrival of a child in her womb.
Thomas renewed the message of peace,
seeking to bridge deep and painful divides,
establishing a new church of reconciliation
and healing in the hills, serving and uniting
the maimed soldiers who had limped home
from battles, no longer wearing blue or gray,
a church that remains today at Swan Creek,
where my father in leadership and in love
sings still the rooted hymns intoned there
by his great-grandfather Thomas—where,
when hearts are heavy, Jesus and Mary
mirror the soul and say, *Let's start anew.*

Thomas traveled many trails,
        but he never once traveled alone.

# Mountain Woman in Four Seasons

Watching the purple horizon lift upward
like a cathedral blessing in the loveliest
time of the year, I have seen my sister
standing regal in her green *summer* dress,
country girl with Smoky Mountain eyes,
who fingers the delicate flowers that stick
to her skin like Monet impressions
as she swims seas of woodland phlox.

And often, when in this cool valley,
I tilt my head upward to the mountains
and feel still the fervent comfort
of Mama's golden-leaf arm
as I look deeply into the *autumn*
fury of her protective gazes,
angry at the hidebound ones who jeer
at her hillbilly girl.

There are times too that Mamaw
is quite near me, living on borrowed time
in the Appalachian woodlands,
with her *winter*-white chill and fallen hair,
shaking me with grandmotherly urgency,
calling me away from diamond dreams.
In her bare-tree limbs, I notice
a strength more forceful than iron.

I've watched these—my women kin,
these stalwart mountains—as I've walked
down dirt paths, seeking my bearings.
But right now I see myself, as I stand
where the *spring* stream gleams,
my reflection looming wider and taller
than it ever is without the hills behind me.
Of course, the city mirrors catch me too,
but they just don't seem to recognize
the magnitude of a Mountain Woman.

# Whispers of Wings and Things

Mamaw was a brave, bright butterfly,
         ever flitting,
     ever sitting,
darting and lingering synchronously,
zigzagging her meandering magic
      up and down
pastel quilts of creeping phlox,
sewing earth to sky with such lurid stitchery,
      darting in and out
of the woodland paradise,
      fingers dripping with panaceas,
celebrating the waxing and the waning
     of purple petals,
     healing herbs,
     and mumbling moons,
savoring her drams of honeyed pleasures,
      however transient
      and censured by others,
      winging daily
in the mountain sanctuary,
bearing wild berries the size of apples
and heirloom apples the size of stars,
      traversing the rainbow for treasures,
hoarding not her discoveries,
      placing jeweled preserves
      from the far reaches of the cosmos

into a large weatherworn cupboard
for little hands to find,
inhaling plum grannies from dawn to dusk
to relieve the toil of gathering rain
in a barrel to soothe parched throats,
seeing visions no one else saw,
coming and going,
mending and tearing,
flushing and fading
on velvet whispers, sighs, gasps,
quivering away with crippled wings
into the setting sun
to find a last haven of honeysuckle.

# Mecca to Monteagle

In a quaint bookstore in a Tennessee town,
I unearthed the obsolete Tolstoy book
that once had inspired Gandhi—
*The Kingdom of God Is Within You.*

Minutes later, I ambled into the café,
lured by the smells of vegetarian cuisine
named after Gandhi. And I devoured both.
After all, books are food too.

More and more, in oracular whispers,
the universe seems to speak to me
the messages of *ahimsa*. Of nonviolence.
Of positive change. Of witness.

The Tolstoian treasure appeared as a sign
two days after my mecca to Monteagle,
venturing to Old Highlander Lane, a path
off Highway 41, leading to the forgotten
grounds of the Highlander Folk School,
a brave haven of action and history.
As my boots touched the trodden furrows
of this country road in East Tennessee—
my region and my homeland—
deep peace floated on the breeze
that still carried the redolent words

of the great ghosts of change, working
toward something larger than themselves.
Here they were again, where I walked,
whispering, breathing, and exhorting—
Dr. King and Rosa Parks,
Septima Clark and John Lewis.

Except for the presence of these spirits,
I was stunned that not much remained,
other than that resilient old library
where retreat trainings had been held,
a place now locked to the public
while preservationists slowly ponder
restoration and inheritance.
But that day, the current owner was there,
and he led me into the empty building,
then allowed me to sit alone with history
and to muse mindfully in this sacred space
where the dreamers dreamed collectively—
where they saw reflection in community,
where the curriculum was their experiences
and the lessons their courage to share.

The walls still held their fingerprints,
the worn floor the imprints of their feet,
the wooden beams the breath of accord,
and Pete Seeger's harmonizing folk songs
incited peaceful protest in the expectant air.

As I was departing this hallowed place,
the hardy voice of Myles Horton—
fellow Tennessean and fellow educator—
droned with the candor of chats with Freire,
speaking boldly to me from another book,
*We Make the Road by Walking.*

# Walking in Clinton

On the good ground of the Alex Haley Farm
with allied hearts at a retreat we've titled
*Keep Walking*, the hiker in me takes note
of the trails this place has marked—
its hopes, its dreams, its changemaking.

Strolling among the salient structures
of Maya Lin, I recall an old hymn that once
rose brightly from my grandfather's voice,
resounding with my footsteps while I walk.
As I hum it at this farm of remembrance,
Dr. King's legacy lives in Tennessee pines,
and we, sojourners, place our soles
on the emergent path together,
compassing toward sun and change.

Mindfully, I trail the steps of the Clinton 12,
those young East Tennesseans who altered
the world simply, bravely, by putting
their feet on the road toward a school.
I claim this Tennessee heritage by walking,
one measured compass point to another,
from the Green McAdoo Cultural Center
to the Langston Hughes Library,
where a room dedicated to Rosa Parks
draws me to books on Gandhi, fellow hiker,

who carried a walking stick of freedom,
traversing the footsteps of 49,000 miles,
enough to encompass the globe twice.

I pause in the reading room, rest my feet,
overwhelmed by the wisdom that neither
bound paper-trails nor structural landmarks
are the greatest or most lasting creations—
it is the divine legacy of the human soul
that persists in creating well-worn paths,
that keeps marching with resolute steps.

# Bird of Bright Promise

Sanguine bird
    the cardinal sits
        perched
on the bare winter limbs
of the dogwood tree, still,
with only the intermittent
twisting of his dignified head.
It seems a bright promise
meant wholly for me,
this creature of lore and luck,
    but I am quick
to defer its gift to you,
bless its wings with my prayer,
    and send it onward
to the Great Land,
knowing such birds won't
fly northwest from Tennessee
this dark, cold time of year.
Still, my soul says that
the sudden flutter of its wings
in phoenix ascent
will alone today create a zephyr
on a woods-scented route,
outbound to the wider world.

# Outbound Treks

# Sailing Toward Shiprock

Like Thelma and Louise, two fearless gals,
driving from Window Rock to Highway 12,
we sink deep into the heart of Navajo land,
singing and winging our way
toward Canyon de Chelly,
passing through Tsaile, sailing our car
through the open range of horses free
on the high desert green.

Then we stand on the rim of a canyon bowl,
circular mandala of earth, watching
the dance of light and shadow pulsing
from the red rock rising.
From a distance we see the sandstone
of ancient dwellings, and green corn billows
across the Navajo farms in the canyon bed—
marks of the continuum of human existence.
But we see no people anywhere, no trekkers
today in this place, no explorers willing
to venture this far off the path to a quiet land
that enchanted the Ancients and Ansel Adams.

Reaching into the depths of silence, broken
only by the clanging of goat bells drifting up
from far below, we find ourselves reciting
a lilting portion of a Navajo Night Chant—

*With beauty all around us, we walk. Hózhó.*
The Master Sculptor took 100 million years
to create this, a scop etching long lines
of living poetry into a grand book of life
that only some will take time to read.

This return to the pulse of the universe turns
us back to Tsaile and then to Lukachukai
to dare the wild path through Buffalo Pass,
an unpaved dirt road sprinkled with roots
and rubicund rocks along a switchback
zigzagging upwards, left and right laced
with undulant scents of junipers and piñons.

At the top we see a cool stretch of aspens,
those able musicians in the mountain air,
so we stop in our tracks to listen to them
play like a multitude of *kokopellis.*
It is then we discover the distant Shiprock,
lighthouse to us wandering wayfarers—
a stone of witness grander than a road map.

When it is time to leave the mountain,
sailing downward into an open valley
of red-rock stretch alongside the ship,
glowing pink in the early evening,
our allied hearts are bathed in new light.

*In loving memory of my best friend Pam*

# Resolana

*Resolana,* the sunny side of the building,
bright adobe in the incandescence,
evoked in the north to shine
         on the south-facing wall
to give voice to the past,
and the *resolaneros* gather to hear stories
in the place of memories, collective space,
receptacle of immense power, bearing,
like history, the responsibility to remember,
         bringing to light
the gold of buried knowledge,
without which the trail will be unseen.

And to know this soul of New Mexico—
this adobe, illumination, and story—
is to sojourn where wisdom dwells in clay,
where the storytellers ramble,
leaving their wispy breath behind them
under layers of place on a path that must be
laid bare in the nimble energy of the
         sunshine.

Reflecting this, I am called to travel toward
the Zia and listen to a Taos Pueblo woman
tell me that the sacred nature of space
includes the pure elements of water and air,

where multi-storied buildings made of earth
are aligned toward sun like a testimony.
          *Sol.* Resolana.
In all ways we walk, we must seek light.

# Dwelling in Cliffs

We must seek stone knowledge of ancestors
to sustain us, halcyon symbols of long ago
that still point us homeward because we are,
in essence, dwelling in ruins ourselves now,
hanging by a worn thread in a dark cosmos.
But the deft language of cliff dwellers speaks
in the voice of sandstone rising from the past
to be communiques in abandoned walls,
standing stories, layered narratives akin
to our own anecdotes of hope and of loss.

The space just inside a stone doorway, with
its ceremonies of birth and death, is perhaps
more gravid with truth than the vacant walls.
Edifice and remembrance entangle, stacked
like prophets to reach upward to us, beyond
the curving rim of green mesa to blue sky.
Those who built here knew something about
time and patience, trusting their creations
of brick and breath might stand forever,
drawing us to shaped abodes linked to trails
in the sacred terrain, an eternal song-scape
of journeys marked by melody and feet.

Once I travelled such a sonorous trail,
the curved loop flanking Spruce Canyon

on the mesa, mecca to Petroglyph Point,
where open and chiseled hands hide nothing,
especially not the healing silence no longer
found in the fray of life, except in a remote
place like this, full of ancestral whispers.

Years later, I returned to sit among stones
for an archaeology project at Crow Canyon,
my hands plunged deep in the Colorado dirt,
sifting sherds of pottery with great patience,
reminding me of the many boxes of photos
and written records, those susurrant stones
of my grandparents' lives that I have also
curiously uncovered, artifacts beckoning
and chastising like a petroglyphic palm,
raised to halt and to ask a stone-heavy
question. *What will you leave behind?*

# The Voices of Pots

As she looks upon the converging paths
of Santa Fe, weaving back 1,000 years,
she sifts through the conqueror's blood
and once again finds her primeval voice,
the Clay Mother guiding her hands
as she holds a burnishing stone,
smelling the woods, hearing the birds,
feeling the coolness of air after the rain,
then the resonant warmth of sun rising.

She feels all these things in the clay,
sensing and unfolding braided stories
about Corn Mother, re-weaving magic
in a Santo Domingo geometry of lines
that will make new rhyme and reason
from clay dug, dried, crushed, and sifted
to remove contaminants and violence.
Adding temper with water, she mixes
in peace, then kneads the earthen dough.

This pot will be like a newborn person,
made from the earth, the core of life,
becoming a treasured part of a family,
then aging and returning to the soil,
to speak in discarded pottery sherds,
fragments that will tell a larger truth,

like the storytellers testify—
we all are the clay we knead and shape,
we all are the earth and the paths we walk,
we all are the stories we leave behind.

# Alive at Dead Horse Point

Stripped down,
elemental,
place placid
far beyond reprieve,
deepest space simple,
standing face-to-face
with the core of the All,
leaning into the echoes
of the divine Voice,
upright like ancient stone
rising from red earth,
organic and essential,
bare and clear,
breath of sky peeking
through terra cotta arches,
sparse but regal
desert wildness
of contours and shades,
whispers against pillars,
layers of geologic matter
carved to catch movement
of clouds and creatures
aligned toward the sun,
free to roam the way
the day unfolds

## Living Stone in Yellowstone

The yellow light from a *Living Stone*
shines upon the untamed wilderness,
depth and height chiseled from force
of wind and flood, animate art anchored
in the groundworks of gneiss and schist,
metamorphosized from Precambrian seas,
testimony to the great balancing act
of change and eternity—adamantine flux.

Even the bison here speak continuity,
the mother-ministers in calving season
stranding new life to antediluvian roots
on the rolling sage-scented prairie.

Along a snowy trail in the Gallatin Forest,
wood songs grace the rafters of conifers,
which rise starkly against the ice-gray sky
like obsidian pylons decked with pearls,
a monochrome landscape of the West,
lavish yet modest, graceful yet strong.

Sandstone bluffs along *Mi tse a-da-zi*—
that fountain named from Yellow Rock—
cast an ochre glow on Lynx and Osprey,
who weave along a river-carved canyon,
their shadows melding with movements

of sulphur and thermophiles emerging
from the warm Calcite Springs, praising
the Supervolcanic Artist who sculpted
columnal basalt from violent fracture
and painted cliffs gold with water-vents.

Sunday morning in this open sanctuary
is made of big sky and cavernous earth,
the sermon echoing in water and stone,
and everything in this resounding space
is a sentient witness of Art Alive.

*Reference to 1 Peter 2:4 (KJV)*

# Remembering Thoreau

Stones stacked simply
    still stalwartly
    balanced and poised
    plumb in the present
    between yesterday and tomorrow
Rising cairn—pieces of the earth
    fitting each other perfectly
    as eulogy to simplicity
    monument of decision
    to live intentionally
    to face raw roots with joy
Elements wafting as blessings
    transcendental in woods
    faeries of imagination
    sarsen strength
    eternal witness to pure being
    to greet life with a namaskar
Gentleness carpeting the earth
    circular mandala of divine path
    rambling loop around Walden Pond
    whispers of truth in the breeze
    fully awake and fully alive

*after* Walden: A Life in the Woods

# Global Footsteps

# Jamaican Jungle Journeys

Chasing the wings of Homerus Swallowtail
and the songs of Rufous-Throated Solitaire,
with the scent of eucalyptus as our compass,
we ambled across the dulcet Blue Mountains
and down the cadence of a mossy trail
bordered by tall ferns, happy in a journey
whose worth was measured only by trees
ornamented with time and Old Man's Beard.

Resting now and then in the cool shade under
the essential canopies of mahoe and bamboo,
we doubted that we'd ever need sun again.

And for hours that seemed primordial—
in a secluded space that *dey road no pave*—
we mingled with mango and coconut
while the carefree vireos and tanagers
seemed to mock our voices: *Fran ya to deh*
we wandered, and *we donkya when we gonna*
return to the madcap harbor of Ocho Rios.

# Swallowing Market Mud

One afternoon I walked to the market,
weaving down the streets of Ocho Rios,
battling the heavens and the higglers
and cast-off mounds of rotten veggies
to enter a gangway vividly festooned
with juicy scents and tints of ackee,
papaya, coconut, and callaloo.

Drenched on the way by tropical torrent,
which had quickly turned the dirt paths
of the market into yawning rivulets,
I shifted in a mad dance from vendor
to vendor, voice after voice crying,
"You need to eat some mango, girl!"
"Pretty lady, let me braid your hair!"
Whirling against fifty-something pleas
that beat upon my soul and aching head,
I strained to dispel my culture shock
and my ugly-American ways, by seeing
myself through a rain-glazed screen
as a bumbling adventure-film heroine,
some Meg Ryan or Kathleen Turner,
in my khakis and a once-white shirt,
dripping from sweat and rainforest spate.

But I fell hard
when I slipped into that puddle—
*wat a piece a rain*—going down, down,
                down from my high horse,
swallowing market mud,
then rising up
to the rhythms of reggae and rain
carrying me to a Blue Mountain road
where my own cares vanished
as I listened to the real stories
of human crisis and suffering,
of interior and exterior storms,
of Rasta redemption.

## Caribbean Countenances

In the depths of Kingston, day upon day,
I regard suppliant toddlers, their feet caked
with the unrelenting loam of shanties.
They teeter outside the sullied compounds
that encage their lives in ramshackle tin,
yet they smile in a way that I cannot.

In the mirrors of their eyes are echoes
of the elderly man with deformed hands
who drags luggage up to the gilded gates
of the Mayfair Hotel that bars his entry,
but still he hums a low mediative song.

The same resolve ricochets from walls
of the University of the West Indies,
where postcolonial poets unearth rhythms
of ancient folktales and proclaim a new
justice rising from their soothsaying.

Beyond the barefaced light of these smiles
amid the struggle, bound up in the cadence
of everyday patois, lies a pool of cool spirit
that ascends the Blue Mountains and soars
and roars down valleys in aquamarine force.
And I begin to meditate upon these faces.

One day I carry them mindfully to a remote
stretch of beach, far from raucous crowds,
walking for a long distance across sand,
weaving a trail in and out of seaside jungle,
seemingly the only human on the horizon.

Suddenly, I chance upon a young mother
doing laundry in the tide near the shore
while her three children frolic in the sand.
We talk for the longest time—she unfolds
her life-story like a novel, and I listen.

Later, as we start to go our separate ways,
her foot dances playfully across the sand.
She reaches down, scoops up a small object,
handing it to me as a token of friendship:
*You take this. It's a piece of Arawak pottery.*
*We find all along the beach now and then.*
*Mi deh touch di road. Walk gud. Tek care.*

Bearing another Jamaican face in my mind,
along with a pottery sherd and good tidings,
I muse the meaning—the holy message.
Perhaps the glimpses of these countenances
merge with my own expanding wakefulness.
*I and I.* We walk this road together. One.

*"I and I" is a Rastafarian expression of unity, meaning that the God*
*in me is the God in you, a one love.*

# Colores Nicaragüenses

Colores de Carazo. *Muchos colores.*
Hints of tints glow on the horizon
of this *meseta* south of Managua,
where the sun caresses the clouds,
prompting marshmallow blushes,
panoramas of people and passion,
roaming in folkloric choreography,
the movements of life, labor done
to an inner tune of marimba players
in a kaleidoscopic rhythm, swirling
dances that step inward and outward,
*rosado* and *azul, morado* and *verde.*

Nothing is dull here—no *gris,*
no *café color,* no hues of emptiness.
Everything, tenebrous or sunny,
blends into a seasoned composite,
like a piquant plate of *gallo pinto.*

The streets are filled with *niños,*
a land of many children holding
*flores amarillas y anaranjadas,*
begging for a happier future,
seeking the Rubén Darío promise
to Margarita—to tell a glad story.

They stand near houses painted
cerise, tangerine, and sapphire.
Bougainvillea braids and bends
upon the walls of severe concrete,
and Doña Violeta spreads a purple-
dappled hope upon the coffee hills.

Market stands are fruit-splashed
with heaps of mango and pitaya,
where the grandmother vendors
wear papaya-colored skirts and
talk of how their brave daughters
had once fought in the war, and
grandfather *nacatamal* vendors
tell of how they fought in the war.

On any given day here, I find it
easy to access the inner palette
because the outer one is so alive,
where every hour seems a new page
in a storybook trying to be written,
where the young are as fulsome
as the midday sun, direct and open,
never hidden behind *las nubes,*
bravely speaking truth to power,
cultivating justice and restoration,
becoming star-cut changemakers.
Peculiar perception paints the sky
gold in lemon sun, banana moon,
and pineapple wind, evoking Eden,
though this is not Eden. Not yet.

But it is a place of vibrant presence,
where neither soul nor *sol* relent,
where *los muchos colores* mirror
the resistance that keeps emerging—
constant, vociferant, forever alive.
*La lucha sigue.*

*For Nicaraguans—especially my former students—who are still seeking liberation, nonviolence, and a better tomorrow*

# Sunday in San Marcos

It was *domingo*, and the village swarmed
with jangling activity, so I took a stroll,
weaving in and out of Nica celebration
aflame in the early morning light.
It was as it always is here in San Marcos,
this lively hub of Pueblos Blancos,
where I can never fully discern
what is being rejoiced and remembered,
but I followed Curiosity in a sinuous route
toward the center of this gyrating parade.
Though there was the same Mardi Gras aura
of other sainted festivals I've joined,
upon a closer look I saw no rosy saint,
no fixed holy statue on a dais.

Instead, I saw the Grotesque in movement.
Figures of death dancing with full life.
La Bruja. El Diablo. A walking skeleton
on stilts holding a sickle—the Grim Reaper,
gleaning the earth with great macabre joy.
These bizarre effigies danced to the *ritmos*
that are heard here at any given gathering—
a sultry, spinning, and quickening pace.
The caricatures were convoyed by villagers
in straw hats and blue jeans—*campesinos*.
This was comic, cosmic folklore in action—

animated history in the present, phantastic
personas of the pueblo's collective memory,
images of evil exorcised and ridiculed
for their toll on the toilers of the earth.

I merged with the spectators, absorbed
their laughter, and briefly sought to know
if I was really there or displaced to a reverie
in some parallel universe. Both. Perhaps.
The dancing of the demons of the past
with the desperate hopes for the future—
where the rooster's crow is tempered
by the crystal clarity of church bells
and the floating laughter of children.

# Iglesia de La Merced

On Maundy Thursday I stood in the center
of a teeming crowd in the cool cathedral,
the smell of corozo pods filling the space
where I mused mindfully, a window
suddenly opening in the core of my being.
I joined the hushed throng that undulated
like waves of one unified tide—fellow
*peregrinos*, walking pilgrims on the way—
moving together toward the adorned altar,
our magnet, awaiting just a brief moment
to glimpse the Mother and her Son
in all their glory, visible representations
of some great pain and some deep hope.

When I reached the front, I was submerged
in cleansing tears, a fountain in harmony
with the floating scent of fresh vegetables
and fruits placed neatly around the sanctum
as a border for the *huerto,* a sawdust garden,
a Guatemalan Gethsemane in vibrant hues,
a fragrant prayer for good harvests anew.
With humility and diversity, the people
had also reposed themselves—their toils,
the fruits of all their countless labors—
at the feet of Another Sufferer.

With no florid tapestries to place properly
in the winsome path of this sanctuary,
they had scattered mere plants and seeds.
They had no rubies, so they gave *jocotes*.
They had no pearls, so they gave *cebollas*.
They had no topaz, so they gave *piñas*.
Gleaning the earth to find perfect locums
for gems they'd have placed in His Crown,
they had fixed more jewels in their own.

# A New View of Antigua

Crouched on the rooftop of a villa
in Antigua—that ancient colonial city
of old epics, old pain, old fortitude—
I hear the ritual sounds of Good Friday,
the processional reenactment of violence
beneath echoing mountains of civil strife,
crimson rage, and gruesome injustice.
Perched here, with the candor of a bird,
camera in hand, suddenly I feel guilty
for the privilege of this sentinel post.
Roman soldiers bolt down the *calle*
as *conquistadores*, publishing with hooves
the primeval abuse of human rights.

Yet, as if by magic, these vanish abruptly.
If only for a day, power seems not to abide
with the dark horses and the sharp lances.
The faithful throng gathers, melded in unity,
around the heroic suffering martyr—
a broken but resolute being who,
without any complaint, carries willingly
the cruelty of centuries up a winding trail
that leads to the Guatemalan Calvary.
The Volcán de Agua also joins the walk,
sending smoke signs to any who wish
to forget the ancient violence of humanity.

*Cargadores* carry on empathetic shoulders
a throne, signaling the reign of a new day
as one single sea of life whirs in harmony
on the streets, moving like hummingbirds
with human hands above sawdust carpets,
some with Mayan butterflies, image of Sun,
replacing cruel guns with palms of peace
during this communal *Semana Santa*.
And the villains are driven out of town,
today barred from humanity's passion.

I soon leave the vantage of this rooftop,
removing myself from the old structures,
recording this on sunlit paper as I plummet
to join the rejoicing sufferers on the streets.
Butterflies bounce around me, birds lilt
dulcet voices, and one lone rooster crows
afar off in the middle of the sun, shouting
*los conquistadores* out of town, vanquished,
and the pervasive energy of the sun nimbly
uplifts the beneficiaries of this circle of life.
Here is something new, and at once eternal,
a luminous and calm horde afoot,
unified to help Him with His burden
and to see His pain as their own.

As I see the crowd, the Suffering Servant
stares at me often today, becoming people
I know, truth apparent in each smile
and shade and pain the effigy wears.
Bright cotton stripes on Mayan children
reprise those marks lashed on His back.

He abides in the old battle-bent man
who stoops to set lilies on an *alfombra,*
the regal carpet for the new Compassion.
He gazes from the wistful brown eyes
of a little girl selling wooden rosaries
to remind me to pray that true liberation
will leap from this moment into her life.
Then I absorb their sufferings, given
the charge to help lighten their burdens,
as I, *peregrina,* keep walking the way.

# Snapshots of Istanbul Amities

Istanbul, bathed in the Bosphorus, unfurls
itself like a multicolored *kilim* in the sun.
Walking the carpet to Sultanahmet's streets
this dazzling first day, I embrace the Turkish
I know and launch friendships easy to make.
In front of a rug store, I yell out "Merhaba,"
and I am pulled swiftly from the street,
seated on a soft sofa, and given goodwill
in a tulip-shaped glass of apple tea.

In the Harem Shop I find a popstar, Tarkan—
well, I find his album and a rad shopkeeper.
When I ask for *baladi*, another salesman
plays the music of Raksi Feyzan while he
and "Tarkan" dance. Then I ask him to play
Kurdish songs, not realizing the faux paus,
but he, understanding, says, "No. I can't.
I'm Kurdish. Back home I listen, here not."
Yet as I start to leave, he hands me a note—
*Seni cok seviyorum.* "I love you very much,"
as forgiveness and friendship float in song.

Strolling the paths of the Blue Mosque,
Aya Sophia, and Topkapi Palace—all serene
dances suspended in stone and tile, pulsing
with many memories of many people—

I come to Taksim, spirited trail of Istanbul.
Weary from walking, I sit down to rest
on a sidewalk stool set for such wayfarers.
A shop clerk comes out with a red slice
of watermelon—sweetness and kindness—
saying, "Someone brings you water
while we chat." He tells me he is from
Mardin, near the border of Iraq and Syria,
giving memory of blue-green beauty
and lambent thoughts of a distant home
after I've answered his engaging question,
"Lady, where are you coming from?"
This day my hills and his are the same.
Then a man arrives from down the street,
having gone out of his way to fetch
a jar of water to pour upon my hands
like a holy blessing for a vagabond.

Another moment occurs today at a market,
where I— a bewildered, sweating woman—
go to buy bottled water. A man standing
at the counter walks to a nearby shelf,
picks up a red plastic cup, and pours for me
some of the Coca Cola that he is drinking.
One more kindness on the carpeted path—
a divine fountain flowing for the wanderer.

Seeing the Golden Horn from Galata Tower,
I descend into a shop for bookmarks, where
the vendor tells me, "You are looking like
my father's cousin from Sivas. Same eyes,
same . . ." meaning my cheeks and mouth.
This avowed kinship is God's sunny smile.

Then in Sariyer, a fishing village granting
a languid shift from Istanbul's energy,
on the street I ask around for a place to eat,
and a woman named *Sevgi* assists me—
she who looks like she is my cousin.
Because she can't describe it, she walks
me to a café, and I invite her to join me
while we chat over a platter of *çipura*,
mingling words of Turkish and English,
neither heard with full comprehension,
still expressing *arkadaş*—friendship—
and eating in the amiable way that Turks
inspire talk, in floating spirals of exchanges
about our authentic stories—our life trails—
in a spirited language far beyond words.

# In the Sculpted Land of Tufa

Cappadocia lies before us like a realm
of madcap fairy dreams, carved errantly
by the hand of nature and human faith,
its light changing in the omnipresent dust
to both estrange the nomads we are and
to call us deeply into a home of stone.
Though the eroded volcanic matter
disturbs our eyes at first, and its silence
is ponderous, an outlandish planet
ostensibly without life, once our senses
settle, there comes the truth—the land is
fecund and laden with boulders of hope.

For food we discover a potato storage
in the cool caverns of Şahinefendi,
where Central Anatolian farmers harvest
crops at the foot of the Table Mountains,
their şalvar legs flowing in the breeze.
And life comes riding out of the stone—
as we gaze on the crater lake at Sofular,
three boys on a donkey stop to trade
laughs and directions for lemon lokum.

Forging on to Derinkuyu, we descend
into dark rooms built stories and stories
underground, where ages ago the seekers
of the light—in flight—delved deeply,
transforming cold tufa walls into secrets,
where Paul and Barnabas educated
the changemakers for a brand new world.

When we finally reach the Ihlara Valley,
its red canyon honeycombed with churches
long abandoned when Greeks were forced
from the natural chimneys rising in a green
earth near a cool rolling stream, all stitched
together like a patchwork quilt, we pause
to absorb the songs of birds, happy to walk
in this hallowed place, pondering what it
might have been for cenobites to float along
on their hymns among the rocks and trees.

Then we sojourn in the rock-hewn Selime,
a place of refuge for monks and merchants,
a camel-caravan truck stop with holy roots,
its elaborate fresco-splashed passages
winding and tumbling and opening back
onto the horizon's sculptures, where there
is nothing else more undeniably beautiful
to praise than the Hand—the hope written
in stone—and I, a scop, am edified.

# Wayfarer's Psalms

# In the Gloaming

You are always there, omnipresent,
like a small boy standing watchful
and trusting, radiating deep light from
widened eyes in an endless corridor.

You fill the evening sky of summer
with a profuse amethyst silence,
and the gloaming over green hills
moves like purple fingers dipped
in communion wine or mauve dye,
grace in a woodland sundown song.

You fall like a smile to the lowest
reaches of the earth when one of us
ventures to stoop and to embrace
a freshly-severed lily that is placed
gracefully upon wet grass as a gift
bearing the clear-cut knowledge of
both life and death in the twilight.

# Walking in Fresh Air

I stand here leaning
into the undulating breeze,
*en plein air,*
listening to melody in trees,
resting from the long walk
to the mountain top,
but so grateful for it,
absorbing the silence,
the life force of this place,
the great lesson of now,
not worrying that I've
worn my best black-buckled shoes
into the murky pasture,
or that my new blue dress
might be sullied by wind and rain.
Just as I am—
solitary figure on the horizon,
inner psalmist,
Shepherdess—
forgotten by sheep,
forgotten by humans,
but never, even in one
minuscule drop of time,
never forgotten by God.

*after the Winslow Homer painting* Fresh Air

# The Unadorned Tree

Obedience means that I will follow
You into the forest and again bring
myself closer to the particular tree
You compel me always to observe.
Though it is not beautiful as far as
trees are considered so, it lures me
now and then to bow at its endurance
and defiance of time and circumstance,
but sometimes it just draws me gently
to the wispy neediness in the branches
through my own tendency to lean upon
something disheveled and obscured.

And every time that I am guided there,
to the roots of this scraggy survivor,
I am tapped ever so lightly in the heart
by a blessing, and my breath lengthens,
knowing deep within that this gaunt tree
is a mirror of some pure and basic truth,
speaking a language meek in its story
of both the earth and me.

# Walking in Newness

As I watch the earth leap out of darkness,
winter shaken from its mounded form
in the motions of yellow tiger swallowtails,
I imagine You, wearing your deep-set scars,
move from death into life, leaving a tomb
to accept the golden light that gives birth
to anemones and orchids.

Today the fields rejoice and wave, abetted
by rain fallen kindly in night's slumber,
mixing miasma with bright drops of sun,
and all holds the promise and the memory
of the blossoming rod of Jesse, the rose
ascended from winter's cold, dark burial.

In me, too, I feel the budding breath reborn,
unhinging the despair and uttering the joy
that transforms the heart by blooming grace
and the desire to *walk in newness of life.*

*Reference to Romans 6:4 (KJV)*

# Periphery of Promise

Meadows are not yet billowing
with windswept
      grass newborn,
but the birds sing from distant hills
with the muffled
      promise of spring.
And I notice beauty
      in the margin,
on the border,
        through the fringe.


God walks in my rear-view mirror,
at times a toothless,
      limping man
who, at first, strikes a chord of fear,
but I see Him
just the same
and know somehow more deeply
      than I can reach right now
that He is in the
      periphery
always, watchful, a pilgrim like me.

# Camping Under Stars

Perhaps it bids me gaze upon
the clear and radiant starlight
that spangles and pulses over me
as I lie upon the ground, quietly,
linking myself and the solid earth
that I have traversed this day
with the airy and open expanse—
an infinite, arcane sphere above.

And You keep that door held ajar.
Even on ominous obsidian nights
when a billion leaden clouds try
to choke the shout of the full moon,
Your voice admits me into creation,
and I camp with the universe.

Eons ago You fell to the lowly sod
and rose again to claim the sky,
showering down beams of love,
resplendent comets forever falling
in echoing silence, in soft force—
the dance of the numinous sifting
glory through the sieve of night sky.

It takes faith to accept a distant spark
when one expects a booming crash,
an up-close sign as heavy as a boulder,
but agape is tender and noninvasive,
whispering in the vastness of space
as it continues to fall, day after day,
upon our waking and our dying,
upon our laughter and our tears,
inviting pathways to the cosmos.

## Subtraction and Addition

Because of You I see the fullness
flowing into the great gaping hole
in the universe that was never to me
an unfathomable emptiness bereft—
You always have been there.

This opening space is a rent curtain
through which You project and pour
the drama of Your perpetual love,
a story never-changing yet revised
by the creativity that You insert
into each and every new moment

by the rise and by the fall of life,
bearing all joy and all sorrow,
every beauty that waves its palms
across the water and the terrain,
every terror that threatens to shatter
our belief in divine goodness.

You weave threads through us,
warp and weft, sunrise and sunset.
And what You deem to remove
makes room for what you add.

# The Invisible Manifested

Obeying the request, I fill the clay jars
with clear, pure water, awaiting the flow
of opulent red wine because I am in awe
of the numinous, of the inescapable,
frightening beauty of Something Larger
than I am—than we all are—
drawing nearer to observe a miracle.

To believe the promise, I honor the space,
remove my shoes to walk on holy ground,
flowered with soft cyclamen petals, where
I am surprised by the brisk way that grace
glimmers and ripples through a clay pot,
the muted liquid presence of the sacred,
the light peeking through a dark cavern,
bits of glass connoting nothing singularly

until suddenly! they snap together into a
mosaic of meaning, breaking some deep
code in a bright moment of affirmation,
as will be seen again soon, and so briefly,
by two wayfarers sojourning in Emmaus
as bread is fragmented and offered holy—
the invisible manifested, pieces to whole.

# Chiaroscuro

Shadows of muses lurk behind me,
never quite revealing themselves

in the starkness of corporal shapes
though they hover, faithful and patient,

waiting for me to notice their kindness
and to transpose their holy hums
into some deep-rooted and basic truth.

Sometimes I sense their gentle force
beating longingly upon my back
as they breathe and whisper to me—

*Turn around! Look at us! We create.*
So I whirl like a dervish, reach out,
touch the shadows, and then behold
an entity of Light.

# Reading Persian Poetry

Frost melts languorously
from bare dogwood branches,
which even without spring petals
seem still floral and alive,
dripping drops of pureness—
clarity in the moment—
as I linger over a cup of chai
and the honeyed words of Hafiz,
whirling Sufi from Shiraz.
Spiraling incense of nag champa
climbs toward the brocade valance
above the open window,
directing my eyes to a crow
weaving the ether in an arc,
embracing a direction inborn,
navigating the sky divinely
like it is a road with all answers.
And deep inside me right now
I feel the sweet sure silence
and the smile of the Friend.

# Mother of Mountains of Joy

Divine face of the past summons jeweled
images floating, maternal clouds drifting,
soft, billowy and receptive, bringing balm
to my vision and my heart, even in these
videoclips of life that visit my mind like
falling rain as I meander a weary land.

Your presence lingers, Mama, transcending
that oval frame of pink light upon a paneled
wall, the silence of that form so profound.
I know that you want to leap forth with all
your familiar bliss and give comforting love.

I remember, mother of mountains of joy,
how you effusively manifested yourself
in each and every moment, a visible miracle,
moveable in your magical manner of making
each person you encountered a gem revealed
anew, unrelenting in your kindness.

You trod the ground with two firm soles,
swiftly off to somewhere with purpose,
arms always laden with fruits of the earth,
a cornucopia in motion, spilling love
in an expansive path full of fire
and whirlwind—a vitality alight.

When you left, silence flowed
into the road where your feet had been,
but it has become my friend,
whispering the beauty of Missing,
the presence of love abiding in absence.

# Empyreal Conversations

How is it where you are now?
Are you singing freely,
hearing the music of the spheres,
discovering that your voice joins
the symphony of the ages?
Do you step now without restraint,
embracing the full liberty of limbs?

I sometimes think I see you move
before me in a rush of wind as I walk
the wooded trail, and I imagine that
you are in the very air I breathe
because you are part and parcel
of the radiant energy that always is,
always was, always will be.

Do I delight in the honeysuckle wind,
breathe in it freely with gratitude,
and comprehend just a smidgen
of all that you now know?
                    I do.

I remember the peace that washed
over you the moment you stopped
breathing that fated day on this side
of the rainbow. It lingered near me

for a time and then left, but I know
that I must reach into it daily. Peace.
And I realize that if you could face
bravely the grimmest, dimmest hours
of living and dying, giving hospitality
to the unknown, then I also can find
the strength—somehow—to walk
humbly and with honor on my path.

# Internal Congregation

I close my eyes against the light
and touch the velvety night within,
smiling at the radiance that gathers
in darkness in a quiet chamber
where my pupils no longer labor
to absorb the intense colors
of the mercurial prism.

It is as warm as a cocoon behind
these flesh shutters, pulled so gently
down only for a moment to enter
the room of my essence, alone
but in quiet congregation with all
the memories of everyone I love.

They float by without forms or words,
bearing themselves only as shapeless
pieces of light, pulsing like the stars
upon the endless sea of the universe.

# Pandemic Pathways

# Dialogue with Dalí

I, too, cannot help noticing, señor,
that the earth hangs in limbo—
a tottering and careening force
in the cortège,
struggling in the aftermath,
revolving around Time
in a wasteland beset by
warped hopes and shaped fears,
parched limbs and scorched trees,
abandoned ships and fortresses.

Survivors in a dystopian world,
we see ourselves
etched in the landscape,
figures carved in trees and stone,
vagabonds on a trail toward sun,
linked by grace to the remaining
                    drop
of water, of ocean, of life.

Three swans swim the foreground
of our swirling, mesmeric visions—
their slender necks curled
in elegant curves of peace
as they whisper "mirror, mirror"
into the life-giving turquoise

metamorphosis
and watch themselves turn over
                    topsy-turvy
into a trio of trunk-curled elephants,
gentleness into gentleness,
mindfulness of Self and Other.

This reflected grace surely shows us
what is still here—is still within us—
guiding our way as we walk,
even on a maimed planet.

*after Salvador Dalí's* Cygnes Reflétant des Eléphants

# November Beech Leaves

The leaves of the late November beech
curl like olden scrolls of sere parchment,
whispering sonorous truths of *marcescence*,
a reminder that we keep the dead with us
yet awhile in memory, and who they were
will linger with us, connected to the living
branches of what hope we might become.

Their tarriance seems a thoughtful gesture,
their wisps of foliage the last goodbye,
filling the open forest with rasping song.

Playing to a crowded house of disrobed
trees, the echoes of coiled caramel-hued
leaves tremble and hover upon the wind,
their volutes brushing against each other,
prophetic song of a thousand rattlesnakes.

Mighty oaks in their deshabille defer.
Evergreens concede from guilt of endurance.
And I, wondering my own remaining story,
join the muted music of rasping survivors
susurrant in a pandemic world.

## Casualty of Spanish Flu

Encased in an oval on the wall,
sepia image in brown-marbled tin,
with handsome face, perfect hair,
and hands set solidly upon legs,
you do not disclose your fate.

I inherited your dignified portrait
from your daughter, my grandmother,
who never quite recovered the fact
that you left her, she not grasping
as a four-year-old girl that you
would not return to rejoice the day.

You walked one November hour,
your birthday, out into the cold,
cold rain, not seeking gifts yourself
but longing to give the milk of life
to your darling wife and children.

As you struggled hard to breathe
in the icy deluge, ignoring a cough
because you were strong and stocky,
having only walked thirty-one years
on the solid earth that you farmed,
you carried the battered milk pail,
swinging it gently with resolve

on a path you were destined to take,
finding the cow upon the mountain.

A day later, the pneumonia set in,
and you could not possibly know
that you were soon to be another
casualty of the pandemic of 1918.

But your face we reclaim, recall,
retell today, knowing that to us,
your descendants, you will never,
ever, be simply another number.

# Passages

Transitions in life fall upon us
like the amber and ruby leaves
emerging on altered trees
in an autumn woodland—
not part of awareness at first,
though slowly turning daily
toward a deep transformation,
awaiting the sudden
        jolt of recognition
as the wayfarer looks upward
to the calico ridgeline
and sees the trail of change,
exhorting a new season of life.

Summer's soul underlies it all,
this remembrance of newness,
as the grace of undying light
that falls upon dying leaves
makes them still appear as full
as the large lemons of Naples
or a decanter of limoncello—
liquid gold, endless shine—

discovered as a dram on trees
in an afternoon walk in the sun
that yields unexpected wonder
and acceptance of the cycles
of life that transfigure us all.

# December Azimuth

Charting the horizon, seeking a route,
we venture out of the obsidian cave
on the darkest day of the year, engulfed
in the bitter chill of winter solstice,
capstone on a number that first intoned
rhythm and balance in the way it was
written on a page before it became
an ugly reminder of double trouble—
        2020.
Looking ahead toward the angular
distance of the Star, alert in the night,
we—the observers of all that has been
and yet what might be—wonder if we
have the courage in us to incline
our sight toward the celestial goal and
chase a path through the diurnal space.
As we climb out of hiding, survivors
in a broken land, our masks cover
our faces but no longer hide our hope—
        we seek radiance.
With hands bearing ampoules
of frankincense and the humble faith
to heal a maimed earth, we walk lithely,
dervish Magi spinning with grace as we
glimpse a glowing orb, the vertical circle
        that will guide us.

Bound for Bethlehem in bleak midwinter,
we follow the Arc of Horizon, tracking
clockwise the pathway from which
the sun will come with its incremental
      days of light.

# Christmastide Matrimony

Sun sparkles on diamond snow
the day after Christmas—
the day after an icy blizzard—
and the benevolent gift of love now
radiates kindly upon us as we gather
to watch a charming couple pledge
their lives to each other for eternity
in this frosty, quiet mountain haven
so pure and health-giving in spite of
the disease and the death that haunt
the community amid the ghastly,
leaden throes of a plague.

But all is perfect in this moment,
this respite to recall life and love,
revealing that grace is still present
and that the Divine Arms embrace
us here in this tiny historic church
with its stalwart wooden beams
and its cranberry-velveted pews
kindly adorned with pine boughs,
a pure green gift from the woodland,
earth touching heaven as mystical
harmonies of a stringed trinity—
two violins and a cello—caress.

Into this serene place of miracle,
walks the gentle and joyful groom
with the faithful heart, returned
to the cold, wintry Tennessee hills
in his Army blues, marching calmly,
sublimely, down the aisle to claim
a blessed future with his beloved,
whose snow-colored silk embodies
the movement of new beginnings
as the glow of afternoon sunshine
decants light into ice-laced panes.

*For my nephew Caleb and his wife Katelyn*

# Sheltering in Place in Sunlight

Hope rolls through cut-glass panes
with piercing rays of morning sun,
flowing ripples of surprising light
on this last day of the year—
an epoch to close with finality,
as if leaving a house for good,
shutting and locking its front door,
taking a sacred moment to pause
and remember the fleeting voices
and ghosts of countless memories,
then driving away, not in haste
but slowly to recall the time there.

Though laden by the news of loss—
stark death in abnormal times,
one life per minute to a dark virus—

still, one glance at an ancient orb,
glowing brightly and kindly, brings
a chastening pause to gratitude—

I am safe, I am warm, I am well,
if only in this present moment,
where gossamer shimmers move
like humming sybils—the muses
of a sunrise thanksgiving
to carry into a new year.

# Augury of the Heron

From my window the rainy first day
of a new year awaited like none other,
I observed for many long minutes
the unhurried choreography of blessing,
a great blue heron standing motionless,
imbued with alertness and longsuffering,
her slender neck raised to the breeze
in search perhaps—like me—of a scent
of something promised, serene beauty,
grace remaining after that hard year,
peace and healing at the water's edge.

Then today she appears anew, making
me wonder if I am special because I
see this bird who lingers more than
just that first day as the light lengthens
and our time in the sun brings strength.
Is she my totem, my friend, my guide
through the wilderness to the azimuth,
a Celtic compass to navigate the loch
like the Lady of the Lake, protectoress
of disenchanted and wayward travelers?

Like before, she is poised motionless
and vigilant for such a long time,
a breathing statue to venerate serenity,
like the heron sent to Odysseus, sign
of divine watchfulness and hope.

Then she gracefully slides into the creek,
to stay for a while out of my line of view.
Later, I see her fly above the ridge line,
with a wingspan that creates expansion
and well-being in my heart. *Be still.*

*Reference to Psalm 46:10 (KJV)*

# The Song of Wild Poets

Words teeming, bound
with seeming
angularity in a jagged flow,
grace the trusting fibers
of cellulose pulp, their landing
softened by the receptive
depth of blankness.

            Thus, I write,
with no great purpose,
no measure or meaning,
only openness to find
that which must call,

            will fall,
into sound and sight.
Automatic spores,
like the thoughts of Yeats,
spill forward to claim
the bare slate

            awaiting
a *white stone* in revelations,
*a new name*
given amid the black marks
scribbled and scribed,
essential being spiraling
out of Chaos into Kairos,
a beauty of becoming,

like a dial focusing and turning
upon sound waves,
                    awaiting
reception to fall upon the ear,
forming words where silence abides,
sending out to cyberians
more than just a zooming voice
or a cyber-trail.
There must be whirled
                    into motion
the sacred dances of creation,
the small spinning of me
against the white noise of despair,
amidst the myriad hums of angels
and bees around the radiant sun.
                    Here I am,
Whitman's pup *yawping*
in the *barbaric* backyard
            of the cosmos!

*Reference to Revelation 2:17 (KJV) and to "I sound my barbaric
yawp" in Walt Whitman's "Song of Myself, 52"*

# Surfacing

Fecundity nudges the early-spring ground,
expanding gratitude for the whiff of new air,
striving to return alive out of the taut loam,
shattering the old complacency,
surmounting a season of dearth.

Joy speaks to buds nurtured by the labors
of the gardener who has uprooted weeds
through the slow work of time and faith.

These active shoots are witnesses of truth
and change, responses to the forgiving flow
of water that still falls even in the hard times,
testimonies of the sunshine that quickens
life in the fetid, latent, vulnerable spaces.

The call to resilient fruitfulness provokes
an animate updwardness, a lurching song,
pushing even the most fragile flowers
through the most obstinate soil,
defeating traumas and injustices
and the rigid internments of buried pain.

Healing extends its outstretched hand,
and a bud hears its voice, raises its head
to make a purposeful rising from the earth

into the sun, to bloom, beacon of strength,
with the forward steps that only a sprout
can make, courting transformed butterflies,
kindred spirits in the wind's breath,
awakened too from an embryonic state.

# Swimming to Shore

Flowing like a holy Herati
in a complex Tabriz design,
we will weave a song in water,
raising our hopeful heads
above the azure lace ripples
to witness the dancing branches
of the Tree of Life ashore.

The crimson pomegranate
will speak to us joy everlasting,
like a ruby fallen from the sky
to merge with the green grass
and the iridescent water
dripping from our resurrected
bodies as we arise with faith,
no longer lost at sea.

We will leave the scales behind,
like clothes too warm for sun,
removing laminas of protection
no longer needed in a healed world.
And we will stand upright
on the clean, whole carpet of earth,
having arrived finally at shore.

# Nova

Mother Spring, you radiate love,
carrying your glowing new star,
your Nova, as your arms cradle
the extraordinary illumination
of woman newborn,

                both she and you.

You also bear the strength
of your own being,
the creativity of your soul,
the blossoming beauty
written within your deepest self
like the tattoo upon your leg—
the face of a woman in a tree—
your geminate heart branching

          and beating in twofold rhythm.

Delivering nascent life
with the daffodils and the dogwoods,
with the rabbits and the butterflies,
as paths of sunrise flow,
you bring fresh hope into a dim world,

increasing the compassionate energy
between the earth and the sky
with the sudden brilliance
blazing anew out of the dark void,
two newborn creatures,

                both she and you.

*For my niece Colleen and her baby girl*

CPSIA information can be obtained
at www.ICGtesting.com
Printed in the USA
BVHW082146101221
623804BV00013B/856